DA... ...RY

LIFE DURING THE CIVIL WAR

by Kelly Milner Halls

Content Consultant
John M. Sacher
Department of History
University of Central Florida

Core Library

An Imprint of Abdo Publishing
www.abdopublishing.com

www.abdopublishing.com

Published by Abdo Publishing, a division of ABDO, PO Box 398166,
Minneapolis, Minnesota 55439. Copyright © 2015 by Abdo Consulting
Group, Inc. International copyrights reserved in all countries. No part of
this book may be reproduced in any form without written permission from
the publisher. Core Library™ is a trademark and logo of Abdo Publishing.

Printed in the United States of America, North Mankato, Minnesota
092014
012015

THIS BOOK CONTAINS
RECYCLED MATERIALS

Cover Photo: Library of Congress
Interior Photos: Library of Congress, 1, 11; AP Images, 4; Louie Psihoyos/
Corbis, 6; Corbis, 8; Red Line Editorial, 12, 37; Lebrecht Music & Arts/
Corbis, 14; North Wind Picture Archives, 17, 18, 22, 25, 28, 31, 33, 34, 40,
42, 45; Bettman/Corbis, 20; Shutterstock Images, 38

Editor: Mirella Miller
Series Designer: Becky Daum

Library of Congress Control Number: 2014944228

Cataloging-in-Publication Data
Halls, Kelly Milner.
 Life during the Civil War / Kelly Milner Halls.
   p. cm. -- (Daily life in US history)
 ISBN 978-1-62403-625-5 (lib. bdg.)
 Includes bibliographical references and index.
 1. United States--History--Civil War, 1861-1865--Social aspects--Juvenile
literature.   2. Confederate States of America--Social conditions--Juvenile
literature.   I. Title.
 973.7--dc23
                                                        2014944228

CHAPTER ONE
A Nation Divided 4

CHAPTER TWO
Work, Food, and School 14

CHAPTER THREE
**Culture, Clothing, and
Communication** 22

CHAPTER FOUR
Life as a Slave 28

CHAPTER FIVE
Healing the Wounds 34

A Day in the Life. 42

Stop and Think 44

Glossary. 46

Learn More. 47

Index 48

About the Author 48

A NATION DIVIDED

Life during the Civil War (1861–1865) was not easy. The United States was going through many changes. Industries were growing and a war was being fought. Women were taking care of the households and businesses formally run by men. Slaves were being treated harshly. People during this time had to work harder because of the war. But these

Union and Confederate troops fight during the Battle of Chickamauga in Georgia and Tennessee in 1863.

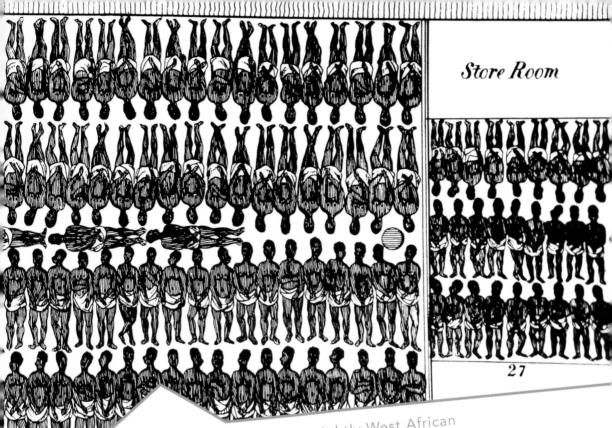

This illustration shows how tightly West African slaves were packed into slave ships headed to the American colonies.

changes and the start of the Civil War had been in the works for many years.

Slavery

By the time the Civil War broke out in 1861, slavery had existed in America for hundreds of years. In the 1600s, many West Africans were forced from their homes, enslaved, and shipped to western countries.

One of these places would soon become the United States of America. Upon arrival in a new country, slaves were sold. They were forced to work for the people who bought them. Slaves were not paid, had no rights, and lived in terrible conditions.

Revolutionary War

Slaves lived and worked in the 13 colonies that made up America. These colonies were claimed by Great Britain. King George III and Parliament enforced many taxes and laws upon the colonists who lived in these 13 colonies. Many colonists felt the taxes were hurtful and unfair. They wanted independence from Great Britain. After several

Free but Not Fair

Slavery was illegal in Northern states. But most of these states were anything but fair to African-American citizens. Many African-American men did not receive the right to vote until after the Fifteenth Amendment in 1870. For a short time after, only four states allowed African-American men to vote. But these men had to own property.

Abolitionists in the North often gathered to listen to public speeches against slavery.

meetings, delegates from each of the 13 colonies declared their independence from Great Britain on July 4, 1776. This caused a war between Great Britain and the colonists. It was known as the Revolutionary War (1775–1783). The colonists eventually won the war and their freedom from Great Britain.

After the Revolutionary War, some people living in Northern colonies stood up against slavery. They wanted to abolish, or stop, slavery. Abolitionists dreamed of a country where everyone was free. The international slave trade was banned in 1808. But as many as 1 million black people were already enslaved in North America. The children of slaves automatically became slaves. The Southern states continued to sell slaves.

One in four Southern families owned black slaves. Some were forced to do housework. These included cooks, maids, butlers, nannies, and handymen. But most slaves worked in the cotton fields. Cotton helped the South's economy grow.

Many cotton farmers became rich. They could plant more crops because they had slaves working for free.

Abraham Lincoln

Abraham Lincoln took an antislavery stand during his presidential campaign in 1860. This worried people living in Southern states. They feared slavery might become illegal everywhere. Southern plantation owners would lose a great deal of money without slave labor. Many Southern states threatened to form a new country if Lincoln had Congress pass a law making slavery illegal.

Lincoln was elected president in November 1860. Before his inauguration in March 1861, some Southern states formed their own proslavery alliance. These proslavery states included South Carolina, Mississippi, Florida, Alabama, Georgia, Louisiana, and Texas. These states were called the Confederate States of America. Lincoln believed the United States should stand together. He was determined to keep the nation united, even if it meant war.

Abraham Lincoln won the Republican Party presidential nomination in 1860. He went on to become president in 1861.

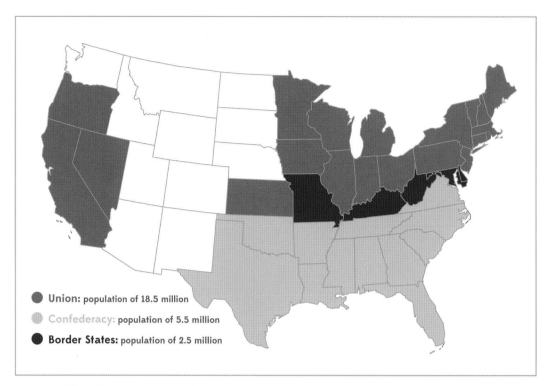

Union: population of 18.5 million

Confederacy: population of 5.5 million

Border States: population of 2.5 million

The Union and the Confederate States
This map shows the Union, Confederate, and border states.
The population of the Union was higher than that of the
Confederacy. How do you think this helped the Union?

Declaring War

Eventually, the divide did lead to war. On April 12,
1861, the Civil War began. When the war started,
Arkansas, Tennessee, North Carolina, and Virginia
joined the Confederacy. The Confederate states
fought the Northern states, called the Union. The Civil
War would not end until 1865. The country and its

citizens would deal with the changes that would come their way.

For the most part, people went about their daily lives. They made changes where it was necessary including in their communication methods, their clothing, and their schooling.

Many battles were fought during the four years of the Civil War. And many lives were lost. But ultimately, the war would determine what kind of country the United States would become.

EXPLORE ONLINE

The website below has more information about slavery during the Civil War. As you know, every source is different. Reread Chapter One of this book. What are the similarities between Chapter One and the information you found on the website? Are there any differences? How do the two sources present information differently?

Slavery and the Civil War
www.mycorelibrary.com/civil-war

CHAPTER TWO

WORK, FOOD, AND SCHOOL

As the Civil War began, the Northern states were experiencing an industrial revolution. Factories offering paying jobs were opening in the North's biggest cities. Most European immigrants settled in large cities such as New York and Chicago. New citizens were eager to work. The North had plenty of jobs.

Women began working in factories as they opened across the North. In this illustration, women work in a hoopskirt factory.

Frederick Douglass

Frederick Douglass was born in Maryland in 1818. His mother was a black slave and his father was a white man. As an eight-year-old, Frederick worked for a ship's carpenter. Frederick eventually ran away and won his freedom in the North. He educated himself and married. Douglass became a leader of the abolitionist movement to end slavery. He recruited free African-American men as Union soldiers, including his sons. He also met with President Lincoln and fought for equality for African Americans.

While more people were moving to cities, the majority of Northerners still lived in rural areas. These families farmed the land. Many farmers left to fight in the war. Farmers who stayed behind had the help of farm equipment to continue feeding Northerners. Many Northern homes had access to meats and cheeses, eggs, flour, rice, beans, potatoes, vegetables, and sugar. These items were also available in the South, but Southern farming practices were different.

Many plantation slaves spent countless hours in hot weather picking cotton.

Agriculture in the South

Agriculture was the biggest industry in the South.

Many crops were grown, including tobacco, rice, and

corn. But it was cotton and sugarcane that made

Many plantation homes had several rooms and large lawns.

many Southerner farmers wealthy. Cotton was used in the states, but it was also exported to Great Britain.

Wealthy families built huge homes called plantations. They lived with their children and extended family members. Plantation slaves did nearly all of the farm work, and they earned no wages. Slaves also handled the cooking, cleaning, and other household duties.

Schooling

During the Civil War, few states had public school systems. Many communities started their own schools. A local teacher was in charge of the school and created his or her own lessons. Students were given the summer months off to help their families harvest crops.

Schools were very small, usually only one room. All grades were taught together in this room. Rather than taking written tests, most tests were verbal. Children

Civil War Schools

During the 1860s most children were educated in schoolhouses. One teacher taught local children of all ages. Teachers were very strict. When students did not obey the teacher, they were punished. Once students learned reading and writing, they found a job. Some students from the South went on to expensive schools to study special trades. Wealthy Southern families also hired tutors or sent their children to boarding schools. Some all-boys' academies had military training. These academies closed during the Civil War so teachers and students could fight in battles.

Large communities had public schools for the local children to attend during the Civil War era.

had to memorize and repeat information to their teachers. Students were not in school for many years. Children from wealthy families could go on to attend academies. Academies offered classes for students ages 13 to 20. These students could take classes in chemistry, philosophy, astronomy, Greek, Latin, and many other languages.

Frederick Douglass was famous for his brilliant speeches. This excerpt is from an 1847 speech about leaving the comforts of Great Britain to return to the United States:

> But I go back to the United States not as I landed here—
> I came a slave; I go back a free man. I came here a thing—
> I go back a human being. . . . But. . . I prefer living a life
> of activity in the service of my brethren. I choose rather to
> go home; to return to America. I glory in the conflict, that
> I may hereafter exult in the victory. I know that victory is
> certain. I go, turning my back upon the ease, comfort, and
> respectability which I might maintain even here. . . . Still,
> I will go back, for the sake of my brethren. I go to suffer
> with them; to toil with them; to endure insult with them;
> to undergo outrage with them; to lift up my voice in their
> behalf; to speak and write in their vindication; and struggle
> in their ranks for that emancipation which shall yet be
> achieved. . . .

> Source: Frederick Douglass. "Farewell to the British People." The Gilder Lehrman Center for the Study of Slavery, Resistance, & Abolition. *Yale University, sn.d. Web. Accessed September 5, 2014.*

Back It Up

Douglass is using evidence to support a point. Write a paragraph describing the point he is making. Then write down two or three pieces of evidence Douglass uses to make the point.

CHAPTER THREE

CULTURE, CLOTHING, AND COMMUNICATION

Clothing and culture during the Civil War changed as daily life changed. As many men went off to war, women were forced to take on more responsibility. Some women still had time for social activities, though. Women in the North and the South became experts at quilting. They would meet in groups to work on quilts. They stitched blankets to show which side of the war they belonged to. Though

Quilting became a popular activity for many women during the 1860s. It was a reason to gather and talk about the war.

Cotton Was King

Cotton was an important crop for Southern farmers. It was used to create fabric for clothes that Americans wore. But cotton only grew in the warmer Southern states. Plantation owners had slaves to pick the cotton. Northern factories used cotton to create clothing and household goods. Then they sold those goods. Cotton was the United States' number one export to Great Britain. When the South lost the Civil War, its free workforce was also lost.

she lived in Tennessee, quilter Mary Hughes Lord was loyal to the Union. Her famous quilt had the signatures of famous Union generals. Even President Abraham Lincoln signed a square. The final quilt hung at Lincoln's funeral.

Fashion

Most women's clothes during the Civil War were very elaborate. Wealthy women wore hoopskirts. These undergarments held women's skirts out in fashionable shapes. Wealthy women's clothes were made from silk and velvet fabrics. Women also wore many accessories, such as hats, bows, and ties. Women's magazines, including

Women pose in winter dresses for *Godey's Lady's Book*, which many wealthy women used as a guide for current fashion.

Godey's Lady's Book and *Peterson's Magazine*, showed illustrations of fashion trends.

Less wealthy Americans wore handmade clothing. When men went to war, daily life for many women changed. Many had to do the hard work usually done by men. Women on farms started wearing

Layers of a Southern Woman

The fashion of the time for wealthy Southern women was very elaborate, with up to five layers of fine fabric. The first layer included underpants, undershirts, and stockings. The second layer was a whalebone corset and a petticoat. Women also wore hoopskirts to give them a bell-like shape. Layer three was a corset cover. Layer four was a fabric skirt held up with suspenders and a belt. The last layer was an accessory. A woman wore a shawl or gloves. Some women used a parasol, a hat, a handkerchief, a fan, or a pocket watch.

practical work clothing such as pants.

Communication in the Civil War

Letters were the only way for soldiers to stay in touch with their families. These letters became personal keepsakes. Soldiers and families reread the letters to remember their loved ones. Envelopes in the South were handmade. Many envelopes were kept tucked inside women's gowns and soldiers' uniforms so they could be read at any time.

In 1939 Mrs. W. W. Mize shared her Civil War memories with the American Life Histories project in Georgia. Here, she describes what it was like to survive during the war after her father's death:

> *My father was shot in the arm while in action during the first year of the Confederate War. He was sent home later because of illness and finally died with typhoid fever. He left ma with six chilluns, three boys and three girls. I was the oldest and I had to help ma raise the chilluns, but we worked hard, everybody had to work hard then. . . . We did all kinds of field work. Mother and me had to make all our clothes, spin the cotton and weave the cloth.*

> Source: *"Life During Confederate Days (Georgia)."* Library of Congress. *Library of Congress, n.d. Web. Accessed July 28, 2014.*

Consider Your Audience

Review this passage closely. Consider how you would adapt it for a different audience, such as your teacher or friends. Write a blog post conveying this same information for the new audience. How does your new approach differ from the original text and why?

CHAPTER FOUR

LIFE AS A SLAVE

Slavery was a part of life in the South since the early colonies were established. Plantation owners used slaves to harvest crops, especially cotton. As the cotton industry grew, plantation owners needed more and more help. While the Union and abolitionists fought for slaves' freedom in the Civil War, slaves were forced to continue working on plantations.

One-room cabins were typical of slaves' houses in the South.

Life as an African slave in the South was very hard. The masters, or slave owners, used the slaves for tending to crops or taking care of livestock. These slaves were forced to pick cotton for hours in hot fields. Most slaves lived together in simple cabins. These cabins had dirt floors and no windows. Slaves received weekly food for breakfast and dinner. They would get small portions of corn meal, lard, and meat bones. Sometimes they would also get molasses, peas, greens, and flour. Lunch was served in the field. Peas, beans, turnips, corn, and potatoes were

PERSPECTIVES

Picture This

During the Civil War, photographers joined soldiers on battlefields for the first time. They captured photos of the war. They also captured images of slaves and free African-American men fighting for the Union. These photos revealed information about life during this time that historians have found useful. Approximately 180,000 African-American soldiers joined the fight. A large number of these men had noncombat jobs such as cooks. African-American soldiers were also paid less than other soldiers.

Many slaves were inspected before being bought by slave owners.

often combined with pork. Then it was all cooked in an iron kettle. All of the pickers gathered around the kettle to eat lunch.

Slaves usually received new clothes at the start of each year. The clothes were made of poor material. By the end of the year, the clothing had turned to rags.

Underground Railroad

Slaves sometimes attempted to escape slavery by running away to a free state in the North. They used the Underground Railroad system. It took great courage for slaves to escape slaveholders. If they failed in their attempt, they were punished severely or killed. Historians estimate that more than 100,000 slaves escaped to the North. People opposed to slavery did all they could to help. Free African Americans sometimes sneaked onto plantations to lead slaves toward freedom. White abolitionists helped too. They assisted escaping slaves cross rivers in rowboats, hid them in wagons, and gave them shelter at night. This network of people became known as "conductors" on the Underground Railroad.

Relationships

Slaves were not allowed to have personal relationships. They could not legally marry. Some slaves were allowed to have children. But the child belonged to the master. He could sell the child whenever he thought it was a good idea. More slaves meant more income for the master.

One of the harshest parts of slavery was the separation of families. Children of slaves were the property of their owners and could be sold away at any time. Parents

Some slaves tried to escape to freedom in the North under the cover of darkness. The Underground Railroad helped many slaves complete their journeys.

had no control over where their children went or how they were treated. These separations were traumatic for families, who were rarely, if ever, allowed to freely express emotions without being punished.

For the millions of slaves in the South, the Civil War was not about cotton or money. It was about earning freedom.

CHAPTER FIVE

HEALING THE WOUNDS

After four years of battles, the Civil War ended. Confederate general Robert E. Lee surrendered to Union general Ulysses S. Grant in 1865. Altogether, more than 620,000 soldiers had been killed. One million other soldiers had been injured. After the war, Congress passed the Thirteenth Amendment to abolish slavery. Every citizen in the country had been affected by this long war.

After another defeat in early April 1865, General Robert E. Lee surrendered his troops to the Union.

A Bone-Crushing Bullet

Until the Civil War, rifles were not used in combat because they were hard to load. But rifles were now mass-produced in the 1800s. During this time, rifles became more accurate. In 1849 the Minié Ball bullet was created. Once a soldier pulled the trigger, the bullet exploded out of the rifle, spinning. When it hit the body of another soldier, it shattered bone on impact, flattened into a mushroom shape, then ripped through the surrounding flesh.

Recovering from the war's effects would take years, in both the North and the South. Battlefields had become mass graves. Many families were unable to bury their dead sons and fathers because of little money. Identifying bodies of soldiers was a difficult and often impossible task. Dog tags had not yet been invented, but the Civil War helped this idea form. Soldiers began writing names and home addresses on their uniforms. Many soldiers also carried photos of their loved ones. Wounded soldiers

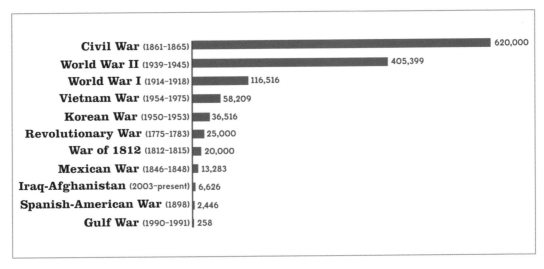

Civil War (1861-1865)	620,000
World War II (1939-1945)	405,399
World War I (1914-1918)	116,516
Vietnam War (1954-1975)	58,209
Korean War (1950-1953)	36,516
Revolutionary War (1775-1783)	25,000
War of 1812 (1812-1815)	20,000
Mexican War (1846-1848)	13,283
Iraq-Afghanistan (2003-present)	6,626
Spanish-American War (1898)	2,446
Gulf War (1990-1991)	258

Civil War Deaths

The chart above shows how many American soldiers died during the Civil War as well as other wars the United States has been involved in. The death toll during the Civil War is much larger than other wars the United States has fought in. Based on what you've learned in this book, what are some reasons you think more soldiers died in battle during the Civil War?

needed treatment and support. Families worked to get back to normal as best they could.

National Cemeteries

Healing from the war was not easy. But Northerners started by honoring the Union soldiers who had died. One initiative raised $4 million to build national cemeteries. Soldiers were given individual graves. Each grave cost $1.59, which was a lot of money.

Arlington National Cemetery in Virginia was created during the Civil War and still exists today.

These national cemeteries still exist today.

Confederate soldiers were not included in these cemeteries. Volunteers in the South retrieved Confederate soldiers' bodies and buried them. Groups such as the Hollywood Memorial Association of the Ladies of Richmond traveled to distant battlefields. They repaired 11,000 ruined graves. They also moved thousands of soldiers' bodies to be buried.

PERSPECTIVES
Memorial Day

Memorial Day is celebrated on the last Monday in May. It is a day to remember and honor the soldiers lost in any US battle. The holiday started as Decoration Day in Charleston, South Carolina, on May 1, 1865. When the Confederates lost the Civil War, many white citizens of Charleston moved away. Newly freed African Americans were left to care for the city. Hundreds of Union soldiers were buried in mass graves. Former slaves moved the bodies and reburied them in marked, individual graves. They even held a parade to honor them. The tradition lives on as Memorial Day today.

Many slaves moved to the North after they were declared free.

End of the Civil War

Lincoln called for a new and better country at the end of the war. He was murdered on April 11, 1865, before he could see this happen. But he helped begin the process of reuniting the country. It would be a long road before the country was united. The South had major rebuilding to go through. New government officials had to be elected. African Americans still did not have equal rights and would have to fight for years afterward to achieve them. Although there was still a lot of work to be done, the Civil War opened new paths for the young country. The Civil War had seen the end of slavery, the preservation of the young nation, and the paving of the way for a free country for all.

FURTHER EVIDENCE

There is quite a bit of information about the aftermath of the Civil War in Chapter Five. But if you could pick out the main point of the chapter, what would it be? What evidence was given to support that point? Visit the website below to learn more about deaths during the Civil War. Choose a quote from the website that relates to this chapter. Does this quote support the author's main point? Does it make a new point? Write a few sentences explaining how the quote you found relates to this chapter.

Death and the Civil War
www.mycorelibrary.com/civil-war

Sarah is a plantation owner's wife. She runs their home in Mississippi, while her husband, Wesley, manages the plantation business. Jane and Mary are two of the family's slaves. They handle all of the housework.

5:00 a.m.

Sarah's kitchen is full of delicious smells, thanks to Jane. But Sarah won't be awake for hours. She's asleep in her thick feather bed, beneath a handcrafted quilt.

12:00 p.m.

Sarah wakes and takes the bath Mary drew for her. Mary then helps her dress and brushes her hair. Sarah eats one egg and one piece of bacon that Jane cooked.

1:00 p.m.
Sarah and her friends hold a meeting to discuss how to help the Confederate soldiers. Jane and Mary serve the ladies pie and tea.

2:30 p.m.
Sarah waves good-bye to her friends. She goes to take a nap.

3:00 p.m.
Mary dusts each room in the house, while Jane mends and washes the clothes.

5:00 p.m.
They dress Sarah in her evening wear so she can greet Wesley when he comes home from work.

6:00 p.m.
Sarah and Wesley eat a six-course meal in the formal dining room.

7:00 p.m.
Jane clears the table and washes the dishes. Sarah and her husband retire to the music room. They play piano for a while before going to bed at 8:30 p.m.

9:00 p.m.
Jane and Mary leave the house to sleep in their cabin.

Why Do I Care?

The Civil War ended more than 150 years ago. But that doesn't mean you can't find similarities between your life and the United States during the Civil War. How does the Civil War affect your life today? Are there freedoms you can enjoy that you may not have been able to otherwise? How might your life be different if the Civil War had never happened?

Take a Stand

This book discusses how Southern plantation owners used slaves to harvest crops. Do you think plantation owners should have used slaves? Or should they have paid people to help harvest the crops? Write a short essay explaining your opinion. Make sure to give reasons for your opinion, and facts and details that support those reasons.

You Are There

This book discusses how some slaves escaped the South to find freedom. Imagine you are a slave running away from your plantation. You cannot read or write. How would you plan your escape? Who would you trust to help you? How would you say good-bye to your loved ones?

Say What?

Studying the Civil War can mean learning a lot of new vocabulary. Find five words in this book that you've never heard before. Use a dictionary to find out what they mean. Then write the meanings in your own words, and use each word in a new sentence.

GLOSSARY

abolitionist
a person in favor of ending something, such as slavery

alliance
a group of people or countries that are joined together in some activity or effort

dog tags
small, thin pieces of metal that are worn around the necks of US soldiers and list the soldier's name and other information

immigrants
people who move to a new country to live there

inauguration
a ceremonial induction into office

industrial revolution
a rapid major change in an economy marked by use of machines

petticoat
a skirt that a woman or girl wears under a dress

plantation
a large area of land, especially in hot climates, where crops such as cotton grow

LEARN MORE

Books

Fradin, Dennis Brindell. *The Underground Railroad.* Tarrytown, NY: Marshall Cavendish, 2009.

Mountjoy, Shane. *Technology and the Civil War.* New York: Infobase Publishing, 2009.

Ollhoff, Jim. *The Civil War: Slavery.* Minneapolis: ABDO Publishing, 2012.

Websites

To learn more about Daily Life in US History, visit **booklinks.abdopublishing.com**. These links are routinely monitored and updated to provide the most current information available.

Visit **www.mycorelibrary.com** for free additional tools for teachers and students.

INDEX

abolitionists, 8–9, 16, 29, 32
academies, 19, 20
agriculture, 16–17

clothing, 24–26, 27, 31
Confederate States of America, 10, 12, 35, 39
cotton, 9–10, 17–18, 24, 27, 29–30, 33

Douglass, Frederick, 16, 21

Fifteenth Amendment, 7
food, 16, 30–31

Godey's Lady's Book, 25
Grant, Ulysses S., 35
Great Britain, 7–8, 18, 21, 24

industrial revolution, 15

Lee, Robert E., 35
letters, 26
Lincoln, Abraham, 10, 16, 24, 39
Lord, Mary Hughes, 24

Memorial Day, 39
Minié Ball bullet, 36

national cemeteries, 37, 39
Northup, Solomon, 9

Peterson's Magazine, 25
photographers, 30
plantations, 9, 10, 18, 24, 29, 32
public schools, 19

quilting, 23–24

Revolutionary War, 7–8, 37

schooling, 19–20
slavery, 6–7, 8, 9, 10, 13, 16, 29, 31, 32, 35, 41
slaves, 5, 7, 9, 10, 16, 18, 29–33
    cabins, 30
    clothing, 31
    food, 30–31
    relationships, 32–33
Southern women's fashion, 26

Thirteenth Amendment, 35

Underground Railroad, 32
Union, 12, 16, 24, 29, 30, 35, 37, 39

ABOUT THE AUTHOR

Kelly Milner Halls has written nonfiction for young readers for the past 25 years. She makes her home in Spokane, Washington, with two daughters, two dogs, too many cats, and a lizard named Gigantor.